97-7574

I0151718

$15.00

THE PARISH CHOIR BOOK

Compiled and Edited by
PAUL THOMAS

CONCORDIA PUBLISHING HOUSE • SAINT LOUIS

Dedicated—

to the many faithful singers in volunteer church choirs all over the country who willingly and cheerfully give of their time and talents to sing "to the glory of God and the edification of man."

Introduction

There are many good collections of choral music for church use available today. However, most of them contain too much material which is beyond the capabilities of the average volunteer choir. *The Parish Choir Book* was especially designed to fill the need for a basic collection of simple music for such choirs. (More advanced choirs will also find it most useful.) It contains compositions of real character and worth for the entire church year and for many special occasions.

Several special features should be noted. The range of all voice parts is reasonable and the tessitura is comfortable for average singers. With few exceptions the sopranos and tenors do not sing above E, the altos do not sing below A, and the basses do not sing below G except for an occasional F.

A second feature is the inclusion of quite a few compositions in strophic form. These are especially good for volunteer groups. By singing the same music for two or more stanzas, volunteer choirs are able to present longer selections without increasing rehearsal time.

The Parish Choir Book also features a great amount of variety. Included are selections representative of various schools of composition from the 16th to the 20th centuries. Some are accompanied anthems, while others are unaccompanied motets and chorales. A few contain simple solos, and one of them is for unison choir. The two canons for Christmas and Easter will be useful in introducing volunteer singers to polyphonic music.

All of the compositions are within the capabilities of average volunteer choirs; however, they are not all of the same difficulty. Several of the numbers contain a few rhythmic problems. These can be worked out quite easily with careful and diligent practice.

The compositions are printed in their original form except for a few which were lowered in pitch. Other than this, none of them has been arranged or simplified in any way.

To help the choir director choose material for various occasions, a classified index has been added. It should be noted that many of the selections are suitable for several occasions. By repeating numbers throughout the year, even a volunteer choir will be able to carry on a full music program.

If instrumental support is needed when singing the a-cappella selections, the organist may accompany the choir on manuals alone, using a soft registration. The organ parts in accompanied anthems are not difficult to play; however, they should be worked out carefully.

March 15, 1956   EDWARD W. KLAMMER

Classified Index

Classified Index

Contents

To Our Redeemer's Glorious Name

ANNE STEELE, 1760

CHRISTOPHER TYE, ca. 1497—1572
Edited by Paul Thomas

SOPRANO
To our Re - deem - er's glo - rious name A - wake the
Oh, may the sweet, the bliss - ful theme Fill ev - 'ry

ALTO
To our Re - deem - er's glo - rious name A - wake the
Oh, may the sweet, the bliss - ful theme Fill ev - 'ry

TENOR
To our Re - deem - er's glo - rious name A - wake the
Oh, may the sweet, the bliss - ful theme Fill ev - 'ry

BASS
To our Re - deem - er's glo - rious name A - wake the
Oh, may the sweet, the bliss - ful theme Fill ev - 'ry

PIANO *(For rehearsal only)*

sa - cred song.   Oh, may His
heart and tongue   Till stran - gers

sa - cred song.   Oh, may His love, im -
heart and tongue   Till stran - gers love the

sa - cred song. Oh, may His love, im - mor - tal flame, Tune
heart and tongue Till stran - gers love the charm - ing name And

sa - cred song.   Oh, may His love, im - mor - tal
heart and tongue   Till stran - gers love the charm - ing

Fine

love, im - mor - tal flame, Tune ev - 'ry heart and tongue!
love the charm - ing name And join the sa - cred song!

Fine

mor - tal flame, Tune ev - 'ry heart, tune heart and tongue!
charm - ing name And join the song, the sa - cred song!

Fine

ev - 'ry heart, tune ev - 'ry heart and tongue!
join the song, and join the sa - cred song!

Fine

flame, Tune ev - 'ry heart, tune ev - 'ry heart and tongue!
name And join the song, and join the sa - cred song!

Fine

He left His ra - diant throne on high, Left realms of

He left His ra - diant throne on high, Left realms of

He left His ra - diant throne on high, Left realms of

He left His ra - diant throne on high, Left realms of

CH 1040

heav'n - ly bliss,   He

heav'n - ly bliss,   He came to earth to

heav'n - ly bliss, He came to earth to bleed and die, to

heav'n-ly bliss,   He came to earth to bleed and

came to earth to bleed and die, Was ev - er

bleed and die, Was ev - er love like this, Was ev - er

bleed and die,   to bleed and die, Was ev - er

die,   Was ev - er love like this, Was ev - er

love like this? He

love like this? He came to earth to

love like this? He came to earth to bleed and die, to

love like this? He came to earth to bleed and

came to earth to bleed and die, Was ev-er love like this?

D.C. al Fine

bleed and die, Was ev-er love like this, Was ev-er love like this?

D.C. al Fine

bleed and die, to bleed and die, Was ev-er love like this?

D.C. al Fine

die, Was ev-er love like this, Was ev-er love like this?

D.C. al Fine

D.C. al Fine

To the Reverend Barry Valentine

Jesu, Grant Me This, I Pray

Words by
H. W. BAKER

S. DRUMMOND WOLFF

HA 2012

Melody from Song 13 by Orlando Gibbons (1623)

Let me ev - er - more a - bide Hid - den in Thy wound - ed side.

If the E - vil One pre - pare, Or the world a tempt - ing snare,

Sopranos & Altos

senza Ped.

senza Ped.

Ped.

HA 2012

Tenors & Basses

I am safe when I a - bide In Thy heart and wound - ed side.

If the flesh, more dan - gerous still, Tempt my

If the flesh, more dan - gerous still, Tempt my

If the flesh, more dan - gerous still, Tempt

If the flesh, more dan - gerous still, Tempt my

HA 2012

soul to deeds of ill, Naught I
soul to deeds of ill, Naught I
my soul to deeds of ill,
soul to deeds of ill, Naught I
fear when I a - bide In Thy
fear when I a - bide
Naught I fear when I a - bide
fear when I a - bide, when I a -

rall. *pp*

heart and wound - - ed side.

rall. *pp*

In Thy heart and wound - ed side.

rall. *pp*

In Thy heart and wound - ed side.

rall. *pp*

bide In Thy heart and wound - ed side.

rall. *pp*

Ped. (32')

p

Meno mosso e dolce

senza Ped. Ped.

dolce
pp

Death will come one day to me: Je - su, cast me not from Thee;

pp

Death will come one day to me: Je - su, cast me not from Thee;

pp

Death will come one day to me: Je - su, cast me not from Thee;

pp

Death will come one day to me: Je - su, cast me not from Thee;

ad lib.

rit.

Dy - ing, let me still a - bide In Thy heart and wound - ed

rit.

Dy - ing, let me still a - bide In Thy heart and wound - ed

rit.

Dy - ing, let me still a - bide In Thy heart and wound - ed

rit.

Dy - ing, let me still a - bide In Thy heart and wound - ed

rit.

Lento *pp*

side. A - - men. A - - men.

pp

side. A - men. A - - men.

Lento *pp*

side. A - - men. A - - men.

pp

side. A - men. A - men.

Lento

pp

Ped. (32')

HA 2012

Praise We God the Father's Name

CYRIL A. ALINGTON, 1872*   LELAND B. SATEREN

Steady, firm

SOPRANO

1. Praise we God the Fa-ther's name For our world's cre - a - tion,
2. Fa - ther, Son, and Ho - ly Ghost, Help us to a - dore Thee,

ALTO

TENOR

1. Praise we God the Fa-ther's name For our world's cre - a - tion,
2. Fa - ther, Son, and Ho - ly Ghost, Help us to a - dore Thee,

BASS

Steady, firm

(For rehearsal only)

And His sav-ing health pro-claim Un-to ev-'ry na-tion; Till His name by
Till with all the an-gel host Low we fall be-fore Thee; Till through-out our

And His sav-ing health pro-claim Un-to ev-'ry na-tion; Till His name by
Till with all the an-gel host Low we fall be-fore Thee; Till through-out our

*Words from *THE BBC HYMN BOOK*, by permission of the author.

CH 1073   Copyright 1955 by **CONCORDIA PUBLISHING HOUSE**, St. Louis, Mo. Printed in U. S. A.

all con-fessed, Ev - 'ry heart en - throne Him, And from fur-thest east and west
earth-ly days, Guid-ed, loved, for - giv - en, We can blend our songs of praise

all con-fessed, Ev - 'ry heart en - throne Him, And from fur-thest east and west
earth-ly days, Guid-ed, loved, for - giv - en, We can blend our songs of praise

1. **2.** *Broadly*

All His chil-dren own Him.
With the song of heav - en, with the song of heav-en.

All His chil-dren own Him.
With the song of heav - en, with the song of heav-en.

1. **2.** *Broadly*

CH 1073

Sing to the Lord of Harvest

Tune: Wie lieblich ist der Maien
Nuernberg, 1581
Setting by HEALEY WILLAN

Words by
J. S. B. MONSELL, 1811-1875

Andante moderato

ORGAN

Sing to the Lord of har - vest, Sing songs of love and praise; With joy - ful hearts and voi - ces Your al - le - lu - ias

HA 2013

raise! By Him the roll-ing sea-sons In fruit-ful or-der move; Sing to the Lord of har-vest A song of hap-py love.

By Him the clouds drop fat - ness, The des - erts bloom and spring,

The hills leap up in glad - ness, The val - leys laugh and sing.

He fill - eth with His full - ness, All things with large in - crease,

crease; He crowns the year with good - ness, With plen - ty, and with

peace. Heap

on His sa - cred al - tar The gifts His good-ness gave, The

gold - en sheaves of har - vest, The souls He died to save. Your

ye fall,

hearts lay down be - fore Him When at His feet _____ ye fall, And

with your lives a - dore Him Who gave His life for all, for all.

rall. e cresc.   *ff*   all.

HA 2013

Hail to the Lord's Anointed

JAMES MONTGOMERY, 1771—1854

LEONHART SCHROETER, 1540—1602
Edited by Paul Thomas

SOPRANO

ALTO

TENOR

BASS

1. Hail to the Lord's A - noint - ed, Great Da - vid's great-er
2. Kings shall bow down be - fore Him And gold and in - cense

(For rehearsal only)

Son! Hail, in the time ap - point - ed, His reign on earth be -
bring; All na - tions shall a - dore Him, His praise all peo - ples

CH 1049   For Advent, Epiphany, or general use.

Soprano/Alto:
gun! He comes to break op-pres-sion, To set the cap-tive
sing; To Him shall prayer un-ceas-ing And dai-ly vows as-

He comes ___ to break op-pres-sion, To set the cap-tive
To Him ___ shall prayer un-ceas-ing And dai-ly vows as-

He comes ___ to break op-pres-sion, To set the cap-tive
To Him ___ shall prayer un-ceas-ing And dai-ly vows as-

gun!
sing;

To set the cap-tive
And dai-ly vows as-

free, To take a-way trans-gres-sion, And rule in eq-
cend, His king-dom still in-creas-ing, A king-dom with-

free, To take a-way trans-gres-sion, And rule in eq
cend, His king-dom still in-creas-ing, A king-dom with-

free, To take a-way trans-gres-sion, And rule in
cend, His king-dom still in-creas-ing, A king-dom

free, To take a-way trans-gres-sion, And rule in eq-
cend, His king-dom still in-creas-ing, A king-dom with-

Soprano/Alto (first section):
- ui - ty, To take a - way trans - gres - sion, And
- out end, His king-dom still in - creas-ing, A

eq - ui - ty, To take a - way trans - gres -
with-out end, His king-dom still in - creas -

- ui - ty, To take a - way trans - gres - sion, And
- out end, His king-dom still in - creas-ing, A

(second section):
rule in eq - ui - ty.
king-dom with - out end.

rule in eq-ui-ty, And rule in eq-ui-ty.
king-dom with-out end, A king - dom with - out end.

sion, And rule in eq-ui-ty, And rule in eq-ui ty.
ing, A king-dom with-out end, A king-dom with-out end.

rule in eq - ui-ty, And rule in eq-ui-ty.
king-dom with - out end, A king - dom with-out end.

Prepare the Way Before Him

VALENTIN THILO, JR., 1659
Tr. based on Arthur T. Russel, 1851

JOACHIM VON BURCK, 1541–1610
Edited by Paul G. Bunjes

SOPRANO

1. Pre - pare the way be - fore Him; Pre -
2. Ye sons of men, oh, heark - en: Your
3. Pre - pare my heart, Lord Je - sus, Turn

ALTO

1. Pre - pare the way be - fore Him; Pre -
2. Ye sons of men, oh, heark - en: Your
3. Pre - pare my heart, Lord Je - sus, Turn

TENOR

1. Pre - pare the way be - fore Him; Pre -
2. Ye sons of men, oh, heark - en: Your
3. Pre - pare my heart, Lord Je - sus, Turn

BASS

1. Pre - pare the way be - fore Him, Pre -
2. Ye sons of men, oh, heark - en: Your
3. Pre - pare my heart, Lord Je - sus, Turn

(Piano for rehearsal only)

May be sung one-half or one whole step higher.

CH 1132

Lyrics (SATB, three verses):

pare for Him the best. Cast out what-e'er of-fend-eth This
heart and mind pre-pare; To hail th'al-might-y Sav-ior, O
not from me a-side, And grant that I re-ceive Thee This

great, this heav'n-ly Guest. Make straight, make plain the way: The
sin-ners, be your care. He who of grace a-lone Our
bless-ed Ad-vent-tide. From stall and man-ger low Come

low-ly val-leys rais - ing, The heights of pride a - bas - ing, His
Life and Light was giv - en, The prom - ised Lord from heav - en, Un -
Thou to dwell with - in me; Loud prais - es will I sing Thee And

low-ly val-leys rais - ing, The heights of pride a - bas - ing, His
Life and Light was giv - en, The prom - ised Lord from heav - en, Un -
Thou to dwell with - in me; Loud prais - es will I sing Thee And

low-ly val-leys rais - ing, The heights of pride a - bas-ing, His
Life and Light was giv - en, The prom - ised Lord from heav-en, Un -
Thou to dwell with - in me; Loud prais - es will I sing Thee And

low-ly val-leys rais - ing, The heights of pride a - bas - ing, His
Life and Light was giv - en, The prom - ised Lord from heav - en, Un -
Thou to dwell with - in me; Loud prais - es will I sing Thee And

path all e - ven lay, His path all e - ven lay.
to our world is shown, Un - to our world is shown.
forth Thy glo - ry show, And forth Thy glo - ry show.

path all e - ven lay, His path all e - ven lay.
to our world is shown, Un - to our world is shown.
forth Thy glo - ry show, And forth Thy glo - ry show.

path all e - ven lay, His path all e - ven lay.
to our world is shown, Un - to our world is shown.
forth Thy glo - ry show, And forth Thy glo - ry show.

path all e - ven lay, His path all e - ven lay.
to our world is shown, Un - to our world is shown.
forth Thy glo - ry show, And forth Thy glo - ry show.

O Holy Child, We Welcome Thee

Bohemian Brethren, 1600
Tr., J. T. Mueller, 1916

Bohemian Carol
Arr. Carl Halter

O ho - ly Child, we wel - come Thee, With hap - py lays Thy birth we praise, With hap - py lays Thy birth we praise.

Sleep soft-ly in Thy bed, sweet Child, The night is

Sleep soft-ly in Thy bed, sweet Child, The night is

soft-ly in Thy bed, sweet Child, night is

Sleep soft-ly in Thy bed, sweet Child, is

For rehearsal only

bright with heav'n-ly light, The night is bright with heav'n-ly light.

bright with heav'n-ly light, The night is bright with heav'n-ly light.

bright with heav'n-ly light, The night is bright with heav'n-ly light.

bright with heav'n-ly light, The night is bright with heav'n-ly light.

O Child di - vine, our Sav - ior dear, Lead us in love to heav'n a - bove, Lead us in love to heav'n a - bove.

To Us a Child of Hope Is Born

JOHN MORISON, 1770

Lobt Gott, ihr Christen
NIKOLAUS HERMAN, 1554
Setting by MICHAEL PRAETORIUS
Musae Sioniae, 1609

NOTE: This composition may be sung by combined choirs. Juniors should sing measures 1-7 and measures 14-20, seniors the rest. May also be sung in G.

CH 1133

Child of hope is born, To us a Son is

Child of hope is born, To us a Son is

Child of hope is born, To us a Son is

Child of hope is born, To us a Son is

giv'n, And on His shoul-der ev-er rests All pow'r in earth and

giv'n, And on His shoul-der ev-er rests All pow'r in earth and

giv'n,

giv'n,

heav'n, All pow'r in earth and heav'n. And on His shoul - der
heav'n, All pow'r in earth and heav'n. And on His shoul - der
And on His shoul - der
And on His shoul - der
ev - er rests All pow'r in earth and heav'n, All pow'r in
ev - er rests All pow'r in earth and heav'n, All pow'r in
ev - er rests All pow'r in earth and 'heav'n, All pow'r in
ev - er rests All pow'r in earth and heav'n, All pow'r in

earth and heav'n, All pow'r, all pow'r _____ in earth and heav'n.

earth and heav'n, All _ pow'r, all pow'r _____ in earth and heav'n.

earth and heav'n, All pow'r, all pow'r _____ in earth and heav'n.

earth and heav'n, All pow'r, all pow'r in earth _____ and heav'n.

2. His name shall be the Prince of _ Peace, The Ev - er - last - ing
3. Lord Je - sus, reign in us, we _ pray, And make us Thine a -

2. His name shall be the Prince of Peace, The Ev - er - last - ing
3. Lord Je - sus, reign in us, we pray, And make us Thine a -

2. His name shall be the Prince of Peace, The Ev - er - last - ing
3. Lord Je - sus, reign in us, we pray, And make us Thine a -

2. His name shall be the Prince of Peace, The Ev - er - last - ing
3. Lord Je - sus, reign in us, we pray, And make us Thine a -

Lord, The Won-der-ful, the Coun-se-lor, The God by all a-
lone, Who with the Fa-ther ev-er art And Ho-ly Spir-it

Lord, The Won-der-ful, the Coun-se-lor, The God by all a-
lone, Who with the Fa-ther ev-er art And Ho-ly Spir-it

Lord, The Won-der-ful, the Coun-se-lor, The God by all a-
lone, Who with the Fa-ther ev-er art And Ho-ly Spir-it

Lord, The Won-der-ful, the Coun-se-lor, The God by all a-
lone, Who with the Fa-ther ev-er art And Ho-ly Spir-it

dored, _____ The God by all a - dored.
one, _____ And Ho - ly Spir - it one.

dored, _____ The God by all a - dored.
one, _____ And Ho - ly Spir - it one.

dored, ___ The God by all a - dored.
one, ___ And Ho - ly Spir - it one.

dored, ___ The God by all a - dored.
one, ___ And Ho - ly Spir - it one.

TWO CANONS

Ah, Dearest Jesus, Holy Child

Canon for five voices at the unison

MARTIN LUTHER, 1535
Tr., Catherine Winkworth, 1855

SAMUEL SCHEIDT, 1587—1654

(8) Ah, dear-est Je - sus, ho - - - ly

(8) Child, Make Thee a bed, soft, un - - - - de -

(8) filed, With - in my heart, that it may be

(8) A qui - et cham-ber kept for Thee.

Christ Is Arisen

Canon for three voices at the unison

ADAM GUMPELTZHAIMER, 1591

Christ is a - ris - en! Sing praise to God! Al - le - lu -
*(Christ hath as - cend - ed!)

ia, al - le - lu - ia, al - le - lu - ia, al - le - lu - ia.

* The second text is for Ascension Day.

CH 1134

Jesus Is My Heart's Delight

German text by Johann Flittner, 1660
English version by W. E. B.

Tune by Johann Rud. Ahle, 1660
Harmonization by J. S. Bach
Arranged by Walter E. Buszin

Soprano Solo

Choir

Accompaniment optional

ACCOMP.

1. Je - sus is my heart's De-light; Pre - cious Sav - ior!
3. Thee I love, O Je - sus mine; Lov - ing Sav - ior!

Solo

Choir

Solo

He be-held my soul's sad plight; Pre-cious Sav - ior! Gave me strength and
Thou hast brought me joy sub-lime; Lov-ing Sav - ior! Yes, my Sav - ior,

Choir

hope so bright; Pre-cious Sav - ior! Je-sus, pre - cious Sav - ior!
I am Thine; Lov-ing Sav - ior! Je-sus, lov - ing Sav - ior!

*After stanza 3, proceed to stanza 4 by choir.

BA 34

40

Alto Solo (or Baritone) — Choir

2. Trust-ing in Thy love and grace; My Re-deem - er!

Solo — Choir — Solo

I have now in heav'n a place; My Re-deem - er! There I'll see Thee

Choir — D.C.

face to face; My Re-deem - er! Je - sus, my Re - deem - er.

4. Let me ne'er from Thee de - part; Je - sus, Sav -
(Preferably unaccompanied)

ior! E'er pos - sess and rule my heart; Je - sus,

Sav - ior! Thou my Joy and Sol - ace art;

Je - sus, Sav - ior! Je - sus, Thou my Sav - ior!

Thou Goest to Jerusalem*

MELCHIOR FRANCK, 1631
Edited by **Paul G. Bunjes**

ANNA HOPPE, 1921

SOPRANO

1. Thou go - est to Je - ru - sa - lem,
2. Be - fore Thee lies Geth - sem - a - ne,
3. Thou art the Way, the Truth, the Life;

ALTO

1. Thou go - est to Je - ru - sa - lem,
2. Be - fore Thee lies Geth - sem - a - ne,
3. Thou art the Way, the Truth, the Life;

TENOR

1. Thou go - est to Je - ru - sa - lem,
2. Be - fore Thee lies Geth - sem - a - ne,
3. Thou art the Way, the Truth, the Life;

BASS

1. Thou go - est to Je - ru - sa - lem,
2. Be - fore Thee lies Geth - sem - a - ne,
3. Thou art the Way, the Truth, the Life;

CH 1092

* Suitable for Quinquagesima Sunday, Ash Wednesday, or anytime during Lent.

O Son of God, to suf - fer And for a world of
The scene of bit - ter an - guish; Thine eyes be - hold the
We pray Thee, Mas - ter, lead us A - way from earth's vain,

O Son of God, to suf - fer And for a world of
The scene of bit - ter an - guish; Thine eyes be - hold the
We pray Thee, Mas - ter, lead us A - way from earth's vain,

O Son of God, to suf - fer And for a world of
The scene of bit - ter an - guish; Thine eyes be - hold the
We pray Thee, Mas - ter, lead us A - way from earth's vain,

O Son of God, to suf - fer And for a world of
The scene of bit - ter an - guish; Thine eyes be - hold the
We pray Thee, Mas - ter, lead us A - way from earth's vain,

sin - ful men Thy spot - less life to of - fer; Thou bear - est
Cal - va - ry Where Thou in pain must lan - guish; The bleed - ing
rest - less strife; With heav'n - ly man - na feed us. Thou who hast

sin - ful men Thy spot - less life to of - fer; Thou bear - est
Cal - va - ry Where Thou in pain must lan - guish; The bleed - ing
rest - less strife; With heav'n - ly man - na feed us. Thou who hast

sin - ful men Thy spot - less life to of - fer; Thou bear - est
Cal - va - ry Where Thou in pain must lan - guish; The bleed - ing
rest - less strife; With heav'n - ly man - na feed us. Thou who hast

sin - ful men Thy spot - less life to of - fer; Thou bear - est
Cal - va - ry Where Thou in pain must lan - guish; The bleed - ing
rest - less strife; With heav'n - ly man - na feed us. Thou who hast

an - guish, pain, and loss, The mock- er's scorn, the
wounds, the bit - ter gall, The crown of thorns, the
died to save the lost, Help us, dear Lord, to

an - guish, pain, and loss, The mock- er's scorn, the scourge
wounds, the bit - ter gall, The crown of thorns, the judg-
died to save the lost, Help us, dear Lord, to weigh

an - guish, pain, and loss, The mock- er's scorn, the
wounds, the bit - ter gall, The crown of thorns, the
died to save the lost, Help us, dear Lord, to

an - guish, pain, and loss, The mock- er's scorn, the
wounds, the bit - ter gall, The crown of thorns, the
died to save the lost, Help us, dear Lord, to

1 & 2

scourge, the cross, To win for us sal - va - tion.
judg - ment hall, Thy bur - dened soul's af - flic - tion.
weigh the cost And fol - low Thee, our Sav - ior.

___ the cross, To win for us sal - va - tion.
___ ment hall, Thy bur - dened soul's af - flic - tion.
___ the cost And fol - low Thee, our Sav - ior.

scourge, the cross, To win for us sal - va - tion.
judg - ment hall, Thy bur - dened soul's af - flic - tion.
weigh the cost And fol - low Thee, our Sav - ior.

scourge, the cross, To win for us sal - va - tion.
judg - ment hall, Thy bur - dened soul's af - flic - tion.
weigh the cost And fol - low Thee, our Sav - ior.

3.

Hosanna to the Son of David

Matthew 21 : 9

BARTHOLOMAEUS GESIUS, 1555−1613
Edited by Paul Thomas

SOPRANO

ALTO

TENOR

BASS

Ho - san - na to the Son of Da - vid, the Son of Da -

PIANO
(For
rehearsal
only)

vid! Ho - san - na to the Son of Da - vid, the Son of Da -

Original a minor third higher

Copyright 1953 by Concordia Publishing House, St. Louis, Mo. Printed in U.S.A.

46

vid! Bless-ed is He that comes in the name, the name of the

vid! Bless-ed is He that comes in the name, the name of the

vid! Bless-ed is He that comes in the name, the name of the

vid! Bless-ed is He that comes in the name, the name of the

Lord! Yea, bless-ed is He that comes in the name, the name of the

Lord! Yea, bless-ed is He that comes in the name, the name of the

Lord! Yea, bless-ed is He that comes in the name, the name of the

Lord! Yea, bless-ed is He that comes in the name, the name of the

CH 1038

2 2..

Lord! Ho - san - na to the Son of Da - vid in the high - est! Ho - san - na to the Son of Da - vid in the high - est!

CH 1038

O Sacred Head, Now Wounded

BERNARD OF CLAIRVAUX, 1091–1158
Translated into German by Paul Gerhardt, 1656
English translation, composite

Chorale melody by
HANS LEO HASSLER, 1601
Harmonized by JOHANN SEBASTIAN BACH, 1685–1750

1. O sa-cred Head, now wound-ed, With grief and shame weighed down,
2. My bur-den in Thy Pas-sion, Lord, Thou hast borne for me,
3. Be Thou my Con-so-la-tion, My Shield, when I must die;

Now scorn-ful-ly sur-round-ed With thorns, Thine on-ly crown.
For it was my trans-gres-sion Which brought this woe on Thee.
Re-mind me of Thy Pas-sion When my last hour draws nigh.

O sa-cred Head, what glo-ry, What bliss, till now was Thine! Yet,
I cast me down be-fore Thee; Wrath were my right-ful lot. Have
Mine eyes shall then be-hold Thee, Up-on Thy Cross shall dwell, My

though de-spised and go-ry, I joy to call Thee mine.
mer-cy, I im-plore Thee; Re-deem-er, spurn me not!
heart by faith en-fold Thee. Who di-eth thus dies well.

CH 1135

Christ the Lord is Risen Today; Alleluia!

Victimae Paschali, c. 1100
Author unknown
Tr.. Jane E. Leeson, 1851

Tune "Llanfair"
ROBERT WILLIAMS, 1817
Setting by H. Markworth

1. Christ the Lord is ris'n to - day;
2. Christ, who once for sin - ners bled,
3. Hail, e - ter - nal Hope on high!

Chris - tians, haste your vows to pay;
Now the First - born from the dead,
Hail, Thou King of vic - to - ry!

Al - le - lu - ia!

50

Of-fer ye your prais-es meet, Al - le -
Throned in end-less might and pow'r, Al - le -
Hail, Thou Prince of Life a - dored! Al - le -

Of-fer ye your prais-es meet, Al - le -
Throned in end-less might and pow'r, Al - le -
Hail, Thou Prince of Life a - dored! Al - le -

- le-lu - ia! 1. Of - fer prais-es meet, Al - le -
2. Throned in might and pow'r, Al - le -
3. Hail, Thou Prince a - dored! Al - le -

- le-lu - ia! 1. Of - fer prais-es meet, Al - le -
2. Throned in might and pow'r, Al - le -
3. Hail, Thou Prince a - dored! Al - le -

lu - ia! At the Pas-chal Vic-tim's feet.
lu - ia! Lives and reigns for - ev - er - more.
lu - ia! Help and save us, gra-cious Lord.

lu - ia! At the Pas-chal Vic - tim's feet.
lu - ia! Lives and reigns for - ev - er - more.
lu - ia! Help and save us, gra - cious Lord.

lu - ia! Al -
lu - ia!
lu - ia!

lu - ia! Al -
lu - ia!
lu - ia!

CH 1025

Al - le - lu - ia! Al -
Al - - - le - lu - ia!
- le - lu - ia! Al - le -
- le - lu - ia! Al - le -
1. & 2.
3.
le-, Al - le - lu - ia! ia!
Al - le-, Al - le - lu - ia! ia!
lu - ia! Al - le - lu - ia! ia!
lu - ia! Al - le - lu - ia! ia!

The Strife Is O'er

Author unknown, 1695
Tr., Francis Pott, ca. 1859, *alt.*

BARTHOLOMAEUS HELDER, d. 1635
Edited by Paul Thomas

With vigor

Al - le - lu - ia! _____ Al - le - lu - ia! The strife is
Death's might - iest
Lord, by the

o'er, _____ the bat - tle done; Now is the Vic - tor's tri - umph
pow'rs _____ have done their worst, And Je - sus hath _____ His foes dis -
stripes _____ which wound - ed Thee, From death's dread sting _____ Thy ser - vants

won; Now be the song _____ of praise be - gun. Al - le - lu -
persed; Let shouts of praise _____ and joy out - burst. Al - le - lu -
free That we may live _____ and sing to Thee. Al - le - lu -

ia!
ia!
ia!

Al - le - lu - ia! *(After stanza 3)*

Al - le - lu - ia!
Al - le - lu - ia!

Al - le - lu - ia! _____ Al - le - lu - ia!

Al - le - lu - ia!

CH 1039

Come, Holy Ghost, Our Souls Inspire

*Latin hymn, 9th century
Tr., John Cosin, 1594—1672

GIOVANNI PiERLUIGI DA PALESTRINA, 1526—1594

SOPRANO

ALTO

TENOR

BASS

Come, Ho - ly Ghost, our souls ___ in - spire,

For rehearsal only

And light - en with ce - les - tial fire; Thou the a -

*The words of this hymn were adapted to the "Gloria Patri" of Palestrina by J. Varley Roberts (1841-1920), organist at Magdalen College, Oxford.

CH 1136

noint - ing Spir - it art,
noint - ing Spir - it art, Who dost Thy sev'n - fold
noint - ing Spir - it art, Who dost Thy sev'n - fold
noint - ing Spir - it art, Who dost Thy sev'n - fold
Thy bless-ed unc - tion from a -
gifts im - part. Thy bless-ed unc - tion from a -
gifts im - part. Thy bless-ed unc - tion from a -
gifts im - part. Thy bless-ed unc - tion from a -

bove Is com-fort, life, and fire of love.

bove Is com-fort, life, and fire of love.

bove Is com-fort, life, and fire of love.

bove Is com-fort, life, and fire of love.

En - a - ble with per - pet - ual light The dull - ness

En - a - ble with per - pet - ual light The dull - ness

En - a - ble with per - pet - ual light The dull - ness

En - a - ble with per - pet - ual light The dull - ness

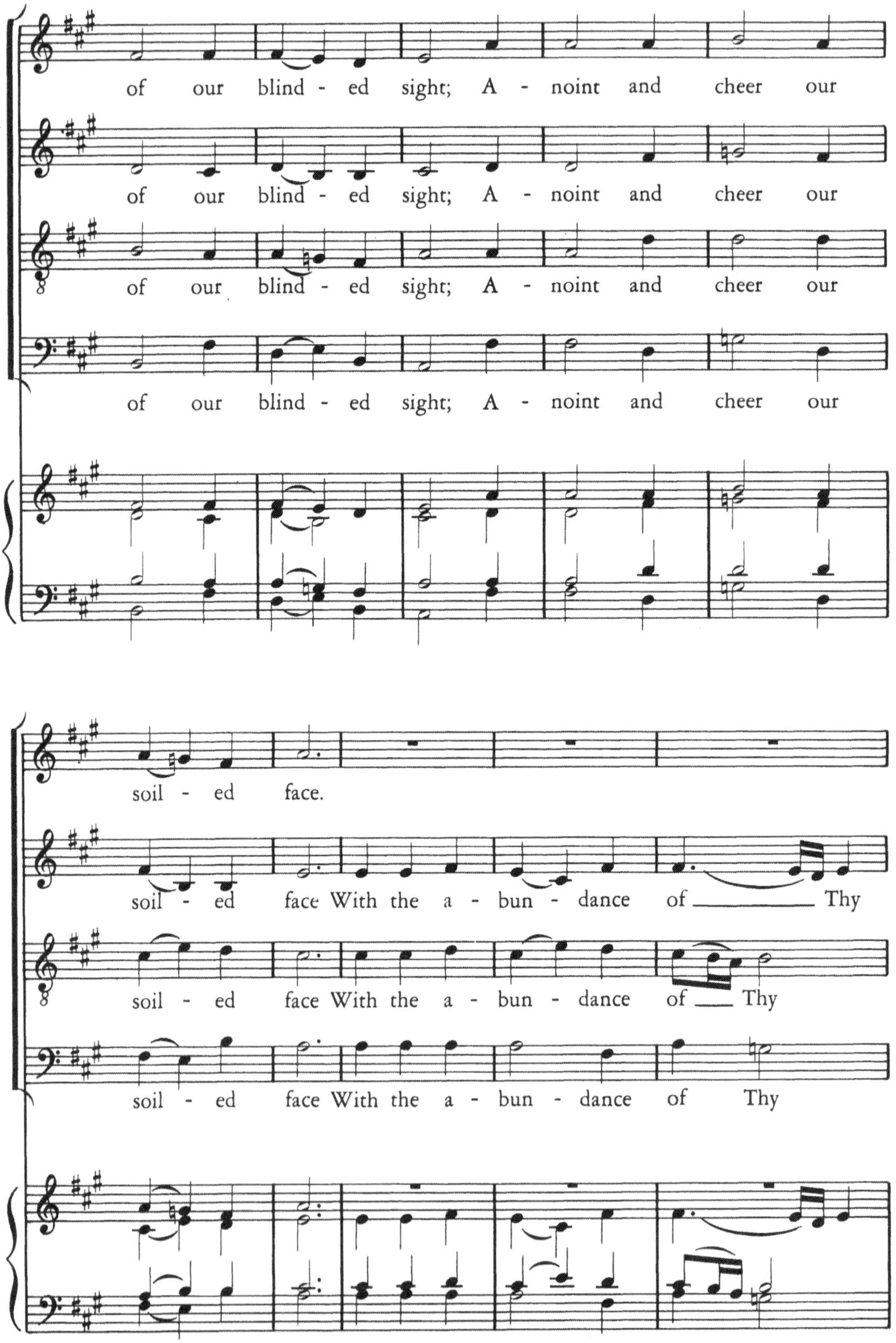
of our blind - ed sight; A - noint and cheer our
of our blind - ed sight; A - noint and cheer our
of our blind - ed sight; A - noint and cheer our
of our blind - ed sight; A - noint and cheer our
soil - ed face.
soil - ed face With the a - bun - dance of Thy
soil - ed face With the a - bun - dance of Thy
soil - ed face With the a - bun - dance of Thy

Keep far our foes; give peace at home;

grace. Keep far our foes; give peace at home;

grace. Keep far our foes; give peace at home;

grace. Keep far our foes; give peace at home;

Where Thou art Guide, no ill can come.

Where Thou art Guide, no ill can come.

Where Thou art Guide, no ill can come.

Where Thou art Guide, no ill can come.

CH 1136

Teach us to know the Fa - ther, Son, And Thee, of both, to

Teach us to know the Fa - ther, Son, And Thee, of both, to

Teach us to know the Fa - ther, Son, And Thee, of both, to

Teach us to know the Fa - ther, Son, And Thee, of both, to

be __ but One, That through the a - ges all __ a - long,

be __ but One, That through the a - ges all __ a - long,

be __ but One, That through the a - ges all __ a - long,

be __ but One, That through the a - ges all __ a - long,

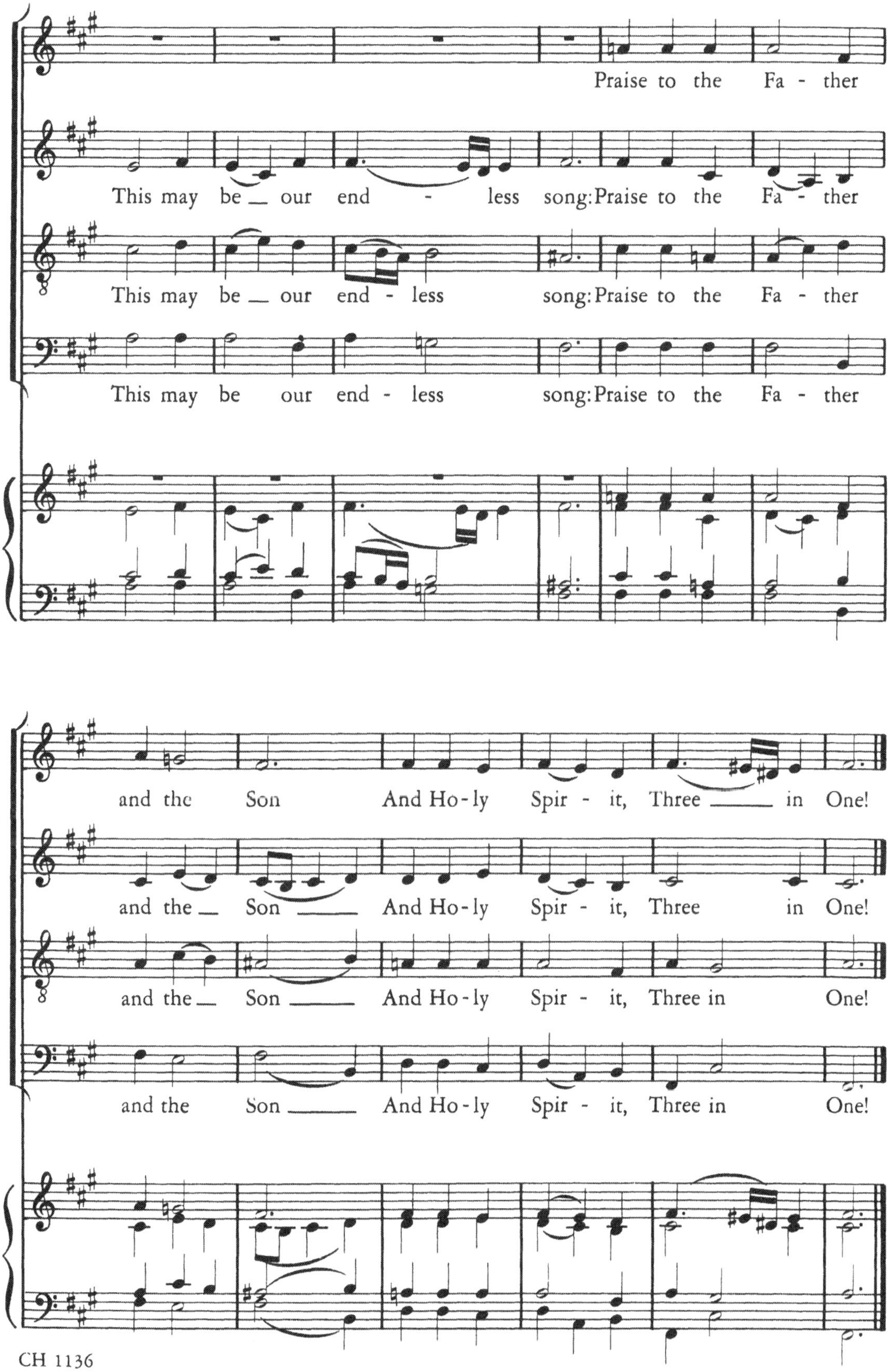
Praise to the Fa - ther
This may be our end - less song: Praise to the Fa - ther
This may be our end - less song: Praise to the Fa - ther
This may be our end - less song: Praise to the Fa - ther
and the Son And Ho - ly Spir - it, Three in One!
and the Son And Ho - ly Spir - it, Three in One!
and the Son And Ho - ly Spir - it, Three in One!
and the Son And Ho - ly Spir - it, Three in One!

Holy, Holy, Holy

(Sanctus - Hosanna - Benedictus)

Lucas Lossius: Psalmodia, 1564
Setting by **PAUL BUNJES**

VOICES
IN UNISON

ORGAN

Ho - ly, Ho - ly, Ho - ly is

God, the __ Lord of Sab - a - oth; Earth and heav'n __

__ are __ fill - ed with __ Thy __ glo - ry. Ho -

*If an introduction is necessary, use the first three measures.

CH 1102

san - na _____ in the high - - est! Bless - ed __

be the {Vir-gin's Son,} He that _ com-eth in the name of the
* {Pas-chal Lamb,}

Lord. Ho - san - na _____ in the high - est!

* The alternate text "Paschal Lamb" is to be used during Eastertide.

We All Believe in One True God

THE NICENE CREED

MARTIN LUTHER, 1525
Translation, composite

MELCHIOR VULPIUS, 1604
Edited by Paul Thomas

us in love   Hath the right of   chil-dren giv   -   en.   He both
and the Son   In   e - ter - nal   glo-ry   liv   -   eth;   Who the

us in love   Hath the right of   chil-dren giv   -   en.   He both
and the Son   In   e - ter - nal   glo-ry   liv   -   eth;   Who the

us in love   Hath the right of   chil-dren giv   -   en.   He both
and the Son   In   e - ter - nal   glo-ry   liv   -   eth;   Who the

us in love   Hath the right of   chil-dren giv   -   en.   He both
and the Son   In   e - ter - nal   glo-ry   liv   -   eth;   Who the

soul and bod - y   feed - eth,   All we need He doth pro - vide
Church, His own cre - a - tion,   Keeps in u - ni - ty of spir -

soul and bod - y   feed - eth,   All we need He doth pro - vide
Church, His own cre - a - tion,   Keeps in u - ni - ty of spir -

soul and bod - y   feed - eth,   All we need He doth pro - vide
Church, His own cre - a - tion,   Keeps in u - ni - ty of spir -

soul and bod - y   feed - eth,   All we need He doth pro - vide
Church, His own cre - a - tion,   Keeps in u - ni - ty of spir -

CH 1042

us; He through snares and per - ils lead - eth, Watch - ing
it. Here for - give - ness and sal - va - tion Dai - ly
us; He through snares and per - ils lead - eth, Watch - ing
it. Here for - give - ness and sal - va - tion Dai - ly
us; He through snares and per - ils lead - eth, Watch - ing
it. Here for - give - ness and sal - va - tion Dai - ly
us; He through snares and per - ils lead - eth, Watch - ing
it. Here for - give - ness and sal - va - tion Dai - ly
that no harm be - tide us. He car - -
come through Je - sus' mer - it. All flesh
that no harm be - tide us. He car - -
come through Je - sus' mer - it. All flesh
that no harm be - tide us. He car - -
come through Je - sus' mer - it. All flesh
that no harm be - tide us. He car - -
come through Je - sus' mer - it. All flesh

All things are gov-erned by His might.
In bliss with God e-ter-nal-ly.

CH 1042

2. We all _____ be - lieve in Je - sus Christ, His own Son, our Lord, pos - sess -

ing An e - qual God-head, throne, and might, Source of ev - 'ry

grace and bless - ing. Born of Ma - ry, vir - gin moth - er,

By the pow - er of the Spir - it, Made true man, our el - der

Broth - er, That the lost might life in - her - it; Was cru - ci - fied _____

D.C. al Fine

_____ for sin - ful men _____ And raised by God to life a - gain.

Like as the Hart

Ps. 42: 1-2

Healey Willan

Solo or Sopranos

Like as the hart de - sir - eth the wa - ter brooks, So —

long - eth___ my___ soul af - ter Thee, _____ O

God. My soul is a - thirst___ for God, yea,

e - ven for the liv-ing God; When _____ shall I come to ap-

pear be - fore the pres - ence _____ of God?

Like as the hart de - sir - eth the wa-ter brooks,

Like as _ the hart _ de - sir - eth the wa - ter

Like as _ the hart _ de - sir - eth the wa - ter

Like as the hart de - sir - eth the wa - ter

unaccompanied ad lib.

senza ped.

CH 72

so — long - eth — my — soul af - ter Thee, ———

brooks, so — long - eth — my — soul af - ter Thee, ———

brooks, so long - eth my soul af - ter Thee, ———

brooks, so long - eth my soul af - ter Thee, ———

Org.

Ped.

— O God, — af - ter Thee, O God.

— O God, — af - ter Thee, O God.

— O God, — af - ter Thee, O God.

— O God, — af - ter Thee, O God.

Lord, for Thy Tender Mercy's Sake

Ascribed to
RICHARD FARRANT, d. 1581
and JOHN HILTON, c. 1560—1608

SOPRANO

Lord, for Thy ten-der mer-cy's sake lay not our sins to our

ALTO

Lord, for Thy ten-der mer-cy's sake lay not our sins to our

TENOR

Lord, for Thy ten-der mer-cy's sake lay not our sins to our

BASS

Lord, for Thy ten-der mer-cy's sake lay not our sins to our

(For rehearsal only)

charge, but for - give that is past, and give us grace to a-mend our

charge, but for - give that is past, and give us grace to a-mend our

charge, but for - give that is past, and give us grace to a-mend our

charge, but for - give that is past, and give us grace to a-mend our

This composition may be sung in the key of G.

CH 1137

sin - ful lives, to de-cline from sin and in - cline to vir -
sin - ful lives, to de - cline from sin and in - cline to vir -
sin - ful lives, to de-cline from sin and in - cline to vir -
sin - ful lives, to de - cline from sin and in - cline to vir -
tue, that we may walk with a
tue, that we may walk with a per - fect
tue, that we may walk with a per - fect heart, with a per - fect
tue, that we may walk with a per - fect heart, with a per - fect

per-fect heart, _____ that we may walk with a per-fect

heart, that we may walk with a per-fect

heart, that we may walk with a per-fect heart, with a per-fect

heart, that we may walk with a per-fect heart, with a per-fect

heart be-fore Thee now and ev-er-more, that

heart be-fore Thee now and ev-er-more, that we may

heart be-fore Thee now and ev-er-more, that we may walk with a per-fect

heart be-fore Thee now and ev-er-more, that we may walk with a per-fect

we may walk with a per-fect heart, _____ that we may

walk with a per-fect heart, that we may

heart, with a per-fect heart, that we may walk with a per-fect

heart, with a per-fect heart, that we may walk with a per-fect

walk with a per-fect heart be-fore Thee now and ev-er-more.

walk with a per-fect heart be-fore Thee now and ev-er-more.

heart, with a per-fect heart be-fore Thee now and ev-er-more.

heart, with a per-fect heart be-fore Thee now and ev-er-more.

A Blessing for Confirmation

HEINRICH VON LAUFENBURG, 1429
Tr., Catherine Winkworth, 1869
Adapted by P. G. B.

Melody: Strassburg, c. 1406
Arr. by JOHANNES BRAHMS, 1833—1897
Edited by Paul G. Bunjes

SOPRANO

1. O Je - sus Christ, our Lord most dear, As
2. Thy watch let an - gels round them keep, Where -
3. So He who hath all love and might Bids

ALTO

TENOR

1. O Je - sus Christ, our Lord most dear, As
2. Thy watch let an - gels round them keep, Where -
3. So He who hath all love and might Bids

BASS

(For rehearsal only)

Thou wast once a pil - grim here, So give Thy faith - ful
e'er they be a - wake, a - sleep, Thy ho - ly cross now
you good mor - row and good night; Blest in His name you

Thou wast once a pil - grim here, So give Thy faith - ful
e'er they be a - wake, a - sleep, Thy ho - ly cross now
you good mor - row and good night; Blest in His name you

CH 1138

here, we pray, Thy grace and bless-ing day by day.
let them bear That they Thy crown with saints may wear. O
dai - ly are, His love keeps you both near and far.

here, we pray, Thy grace and bless-ing day by day.
let them bear That they Thy crown with saints may wear. O
dai - ly are, His love keeps you both near and far.

Je - su, Lord Di-vine, Thy face ____ up - on them shine!

Je - su, Lord Di-vine, Thy face ____ up - on them shine!

CH 1138

Teach Me, O Lord

Psalm 119 : 33

THOMAS ATTWOOD
1765-1838

Note: This anthem may be sung unaccompanied.
98-1343

I _ shall keep _ it un - to the end, and

I shall keep _ it un - to the end, and I shall keep it, and

I shall keep _ it un - to the end, and I shall keep it, and

I _ shall keep _ it un - to the end, and I shall keep _ it,

Man.

I shall keep _ it, and I _ shall keep it un - to _ the end.

I shall keep it, and I _ shall keep it un - to the _ end, and

I shall keep it, and I shall keep it un - to the end, and

and I shall keep it un - to the end, and

p

Ped.   Man.

Teach me, O Lord,

I __ shall keep it un - to __ the __ end. Teach me, O

I shall keep it un - to the end. Teach me, O

I __ shall keep it un - to the end. Teach me, O

mf

Ped.

teach me, O Lord, the way of Thy stat-utes, shall keep it,

Lord, O Lord, the way of Thy stat-utes, shall keep it,

Lord, O Lord, the way of Thy stat-utes, and I shall keep it, and

Lord, O Lord, the way of Thy stat-utes, shall keep it,

shall keep it, and I shall keep it un-to_ the ___ end, ___ shall

shall keep it, shall keep it un-to the end, ___ shall

I shall keep it, shall keep it un-to the end, ___ shall

shall keep it, and I shall

keep it un-to ___ the _ end, un-to _ the _ end.

keep it un-to the end, un-to the end.

keep it un-to the end, un-to the end.

keep it un-to the end, un-to _ the _ end.

RECOMMENDED COLLECTIONS

For Choirs Lacking Tenors

THE SAB CHORALE BOOK

Edited by Paul Thomas

For Choirs Requiring Unison Music

THE MORNING STAR CHOIR BOOK

Edited by Paul Thomas

For More Advanced Mixed Choirs

THE PARISH CHOIR BOOK

Edited by Paul Thomas

LIFT UP YOUR HEARTS

Edited by Paul Bunjes

CONCORDIA PUBLISHING HOUSE

SAINT LOUIS, MISSOURI

www.ingramcontent.com/pod-product-compliance
Lightning Source LLC
Chambersburg PA
CBHW050906100426
42737CB00048B/3230